SHANNON VAN DEN BERG
ARTWORK BY STEPHANIE WICKER-CAMPBELL

CREATRIX AWAKENED

Invocations, Practices and Portals to Activate the Creatrix Within

PUBLISHED BY MUSE ORACLE PRESS PTY LTD

Creatrix Awakened Journal: Invocations, Practices and Portals to Activate the Creatrix Within

Published by Muse Oracle Press Pty Ltd

Designed by Stephanie Wicker-Campbell

Printed in China

Distributed by Red Wheel Weiser

ISBN: 978-1-7635869-6-3

Legal Disclaimer:
The information contained in this journal is for general guidance and entertainment purposes only. It does not constitute financial, legal, or professional advice. Readers are encouraged to seek independent advice from qualified professionals regarding their specific situations. The authors, publisher, and contributors disclaim any liability arising directly or indirectly from the use of this journal or the information contained herein. By purchasing and using this journal, you acknowledge and agree to these terms and conditions.

For more information, visit: https://museoraclepress.com/

"Creatrix, you are the wild pulse of the cosmos made flesh—a visionary, a vessel, a revolution in motion. You birth beauty, blaze new paths, and bend timelines with your voice, your presence, your pen.

This journal is your sacred ground where your wisdom returns, your truth ignites and your legacy anchors.

You are not broken; you are blooming. You are not behind; you are becoming. Trust the fire within. The world is waiting for your medicine."

For every rising Creatrix - in honor of your courage and heart to return to power, reclaim your voice, and create from sacred truth.

Pair this journal with the Creatrix Awakened Oracle Deck, your sacred companion for deeper insight, energetic alignment, and soul-led leadership. Each card is a portal, a frequency, a fierce remembrance of who you are and what you came here to birth. Designed to mirror the themes of this journal—Rooted, Liberated, Expressed, and Fierce—the deck guides you through initiations, revelations, and next-level embodiment. Use them together as your daily practice, your ritual anchor, and your creative catalyst. If you're ready to lead, rise, and rewire the world through your presence, this deck belongs on your altar. Your legacy is calling.

Exclusive Activation Audios and Bonus Card Spreads

Meet the Featured Authors of the Creatrix Awakened Oracle Deck and get access to your free creatrix activation gifts to deepen your journey with this journal at www.shannonvandenberg.com/creatrixactivations

Welcome, Creatrix

This journal is a tool for reflection. It is a living, breathing transmission. A mirror. A map. A revolutionary invitation.

You hold in your hands a sacred companion for the wild, cyclical, and deeply courageous path of returning to yourself. A space to soften and rise. To unearth your voice, your vision, and your energetic blueprint for leadership in this shifting world.

This journal was born from the same energetic current that birthed the first-of-its-kind Creatrix Awakened Oracle Deck, written to access the wisdom to awaken your inner creatrix. It's a vibrational field. It's encoded with remembrance.

Whether you are here to write your story, dream your next evolution, or simply return to yourself more fully - this is your space. Come as you are. Let the pages witness you.

This journal is broken into four chapters: Rooted, Liberated, Expressed, and Fierce. Each one holds its own energy, medicine, and invitations. Below, you'll find a brief portal into each phase of your journey. Let these words meet you where you are, and carry you forward where you're going.

ROOTED: The Return Home

This chapter is a reclamation. Not the soft kind. The bone-deep kind. To be rooted is not to settle or shrink - it's to rise from wholeness. It's to remember your essence, your ground, your sacred yes and sovereign no.

These pages will ask you to return to your body as altar. To bring home the parts of you that have been exiled, silenced, or forgotten. To take radical ownership of your needs, your rhythms, and your relationship to the earth and your own being.

In a world that profits from your disconnection, rooting down is an act of resistance. It's how you begin to walk as the creator of your life, not the reactor.

You might cry here. You might rage. You might finally feel the relief of being held. And you will rise with both feet planted.

LIBERATED: The Shedding of Skins

Liberation is a process of unbecoming what you were never meant to carry. In this chapter, you will be invited to explore the fears, patterns, and conditioning that have kept you bound. You'll meet the voices that said "too much," "not enough," "stay small." And you'll have the chance to thank them, release them, and write a new narrative.

Liberation is not about fixing yourself. It is about remembering that you were never broken. Here, you get to be honest. Uncensored. Here, your rawness is holy. This section is meant to catalyze release, embodiment, and deep compassion. Let it show you the places where you've withheld your power. Let it support you as you burn down the old stories and walk barefoot through the ashes - lighter, truer, and more whole.

Liberation is not a one-time event. It is a devotion. And you are ready.

EXPRESSED: The Unveiling of Your Voice

Your voice is sacred technology. In this chapter, we meet the part of you that has something to say. To sing. To write. To offer. Expression is how we commune with the divine. It's how we take up space as art, as truth, as medicine.

But first, you must choose to be seen.

This section is an invitation to dissolve the fears of visibility, to meet the vulnerability of sharing, and to tap into the pure current of your soul's message. Whether it comes through words, movement, imagery, or silence, your expression is needed now.

You will find journaling prompts that explore your relationship to truth, audience, creativity, and legacy. You will be asked to risk. To play. To trust the voice that wants out. Because when one woman speaks her truth, the collective frequency rises. Let this chapter be your microphone. Let it be your altar.

FIERCE: The Threshold of Legacy

Now it gets big.

The final chapter is not the end. It is the beginning of your legacy. And legacy is not what you leave behind. It's what you live, right now.

To be fierce is not to be hard. It is to be clear. Aligned. Unapologetic in your devotion to who you are becoming.

This chapter asks more of you. More truth. More courage. More self-leadership. It invites you to burn down the fear of being too much. To stop waiting to be chosen. To claim your voice, your presence, and your impact as sacred disruption.
Legacy lives in how you mother. How you serve. How you speak when silence would be safer. How you embody your frequency.

These pages hold prompts and activations for your next evolution. Your movement. Your boldness. Your embodiment of the future you are here to create.

Because when we root, liberate, express, and lead from our fiercest truth, we don't just shift our lives. We shift the world.

Welcome to the threshold, Creatrix. Your journey begins.

Activating the Journey

This journal is not a checklist. It is not something to get through. It is a living altar, a sacred space, a spiral of remembrance. This is a space for the woman reclaiming her voice, power, rhythm, and sacred role in the birthing of a New Earth. You don't fill it in. You enter it. You move with it. You become through it.

Each chapter of the Creatrix Awakened Journal is a frequency field designed to activate a specific aspect of your cyclical evolution. These four chapters - Rooted, Liberated, Expressed, and Fierce - are not linear stages. They are living portals that you will return to again and again, at deeper and deeper levels. Like the seasons, they repeat. Like the spiral, they expand.

Each chapter contains:

- An Invitation to initiate and awaken the phase
- Introspective prompts to guide your inner excavation
- Mantras to rewire your frequency and amplify your voice
- Prayers and invocations to call in support and presence
- Portals to archetypes and ascended masters
- A Creatrix Story to ground the wisdom in real experience

These elements are curated to meet you where you are. There is no "start here, end there" in this work. You begin where your energy pulls you. That might be in Rooted. It might be Fierce. It might be the one section you're most resistant to, which is usually exactly where your breakthrough lives.

The Cyclical Nature of Transformation

This journal honors the truth that transformation is not linear. The Creatrix does not grow in straight lines. She spirals. She remembers in layers. She revisits stories to meet them from new timelines. Each time you circle back, you do so with new frequency, new embodiment, new wisdom.

This is not failure. This is mastery.

You may use this journal over a lunar cycle, a season, or longer. You may spend days in one chapter and return years later to find new truths waiting. You are not meant to complete it in order. You are meant to co-create with it, letting it hold space for your rebirth again and again.

Embracing the Journey

This is a living process. A remembering. You may meet resistance. You may feel overwhelmed. You may feel exhilarated. Let all of it be part of your becoming. This is not about being perfect. It's about being real.

Let this be your permission slip to:

- Be messy
- Be raw
- Ask better questions
- Circle back
- Tell the truth
- Be seen by yourself
- Reclaim your power

This journal is not here to fix you. It is here to mirror you and ignite you. To ask you to return to your own truth. To remember who you are beneath the roles and noise. And to create from that place.

Write in the margins. Cross things out. Dog-ear pages. Add your own rituals, questions, and intentions. Come back to the pages that feel alive. Let this book be your witness, your cauldron, your canvas.

Make It Yours

This is your journal. Make it holy. Make it honest.

Make it yours.

Light a candle before you write. Place it on your altar. Include your avatar card. Come back to this space often. Let it reflect your growth. Let it anchor your power. Let it hold your deepest becoming.

You don't have to be ready.

You just have to be willing.

Here we go, love. Pen in hand. Heart wide open.

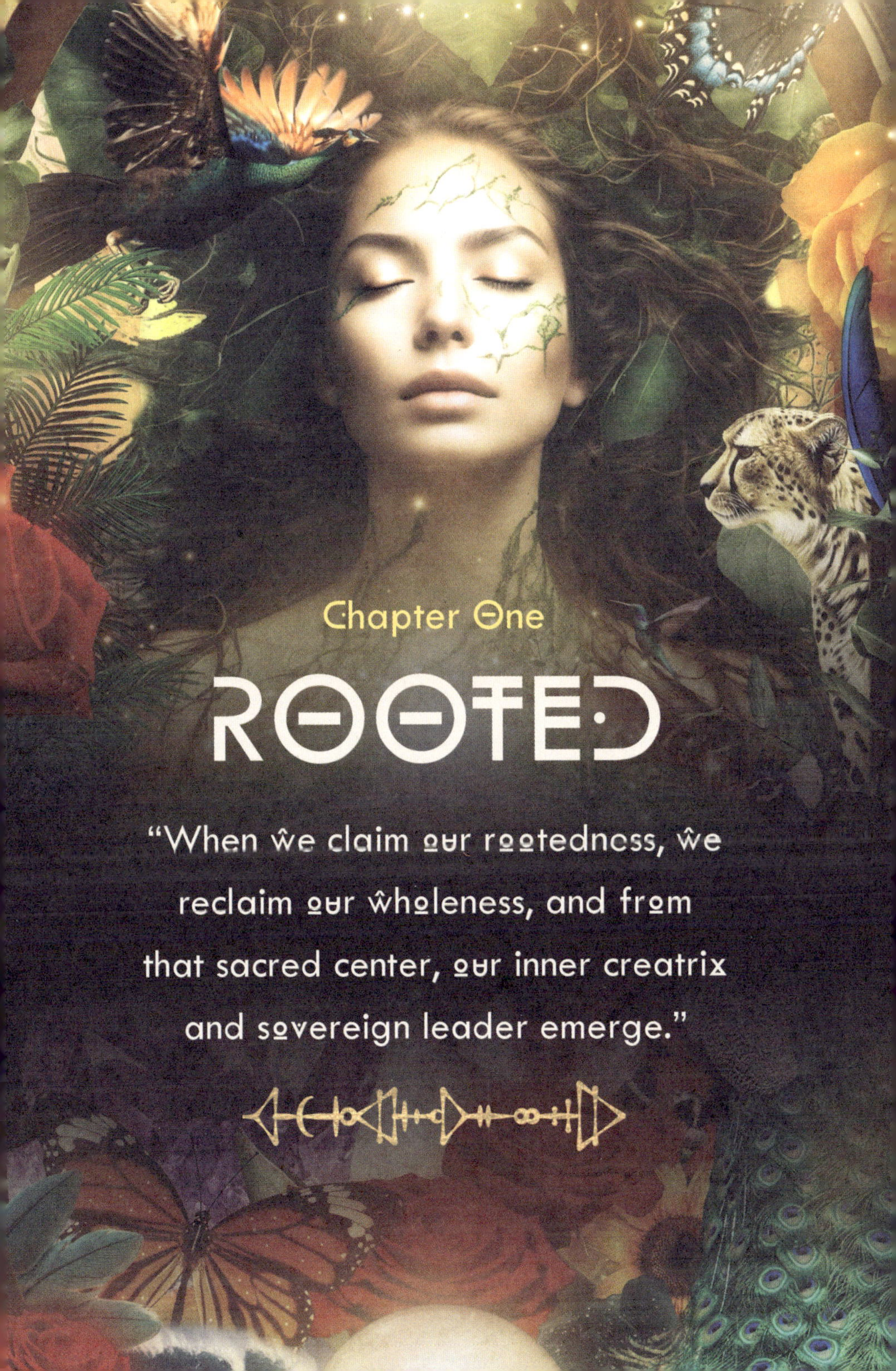

Chapter One

ROOTED

"When we claim our rootedness, we reclaim our wholeness, and from that sacred center, our inner creatrix and sovereign leader emerge."

PRAYER OF ROOTED POWER

I return to the Earth, my first mother.

I offer the false to the fire.

I reclaim my body, my voice, my soul.

Rooted in truth, I rise unshakable.

I am the living temple.

I am the fierce creatrix.

It is time.

I remember.

I lead.

THE INVITATION

Let's get real. Let's talk about what being rooted actually means. This isn't a sweet, pretty affirmation or a gentle nudge. This is a reckoning. This is about calling all your parts back, every voice you silenced, every wild piece you shoved in a corner, every sacred ember you let smolder instead of burn. It's about coming home to yourself. Finally. Fiercely. Irrevocably.

Your body is not just a vehicle. Your body is your temple, your holy ground, the living altar of your soul's presence here on Earth. And yet, we have been trained and programmed to turn away from Her. To turn away from ourselves. Especially as women, we have been taught to minimize our needs, silence our instincts, and contort ourselves into something expected. Enough. This is where that ends.

Rootedness might not sound flashy. It might not sound sexy. But make no mistake: Rootedness is the portal. It's the place where the arrow begins to pull back before it's launched. It's the dark, potent earth where your truest magic takes root before it turns into beauty and blooms.

If you've been hustling, crossing off every item on your to-do list, taking all the right actions, and still wondering why it's not landing, why it's not flowing, this is your answer. It's not about doing more. It's about coming home. Rooting is radical because it demands intimacy. It demands raw honesty. It demands that you meet yourself where you've abandoned yourself. And when you do, when you truly land inside your own skin, the world shifts. The tide turns. The quantum leaps begin.

I know this because I've lived it. I know what it's like to be untethered, chasing every next thing, thinking that something will finally make it happen. And I know the ferocity it takes to stop running, to turn inward, and to recreate yourself from the inside out. Rooting is sexy because wholeness is the answer. There is nothing, nothing more magnetic than a woman who belongs to herself.

Your roots connect you to everything: To Gaia Sophia, our

living, breathing planet. To your soul's deepest memories. To your true medicine, your voice, your wild, untamable light. Rooting gives you your center. Your grounded knowing. Your full-spectrum self. And from that rootedness, creation becomes inevitable. Leadership becomes natural. Expression becomes unstoppable.

When I first started teaching this work over two decades ago, it was wildly against the grain. Back then, everyone was talking about ascension, about leaving their bodies, escaping the Earth, bypassing the messiness of being human. And there I was, standing on stages, fierce and audacious, telling a different truth: We can only ascend as far as we are willing to root.

Without roots, all the cosmic connection in the world is nothing but spiritual cotton candy—sweet, fleeting, and empty. True power, the kind that births movements, the kind that cracks open new realities, rises up from the depths. It is embodied. It is earthed. It is rooted.

And yes, there will be resistance. Because rooting threatens every program you've ever absorbed about who you're supposed to be. It asks you to accept every part of yourself you were told to hide. It asks you to sit in your truth, vulnerable, unmasked. It asks you to see yourself, wholly, wildly, tenderly, and claim it all.

When we do this, when we finally stop escaping and start belonging to ourselves, we awaken something ancient inside us. The wisdom of Inanna, Queen of Heaven. The flame of Brigid, Goddess of Fire. The truth of our inner Lineage Disruptor. The power of Feminine Fire. The heartbeat of Mother Earth herself. The fierce, sacred lineage of the New Earth is woven into our blood.

It's through this rootedness that you tap into the real light, the real power, the real leadership you came here to embody. It's where the fertile ground of creation meets the transformative fire of purpose. We call on two elemental forces to guide us here: Fire and Earth.

Fire, the purifier, the alchemist, the absolute destroyer of old stories that no longer serve. Earth, the holder, the nurturer, the great womb that receives us and births anew. Grandfather Fire burns away what you are not. Mother Earth holds you steady as you remember what you are.

This is no surface-level journey. This is deep excavation. This is undoing generations of contraction and reclaiming the wild fullness of who you truly are. You will confront old identities, the good girl, the people-pleaser, the silent one. You will feel the mask crack and fall away. You will grieve, rage, tremble. You will birth yourself again, rooted in something unshakable: your own heart and soul.

Every woman I've ever seen truly root into herself has unleashed a revolution. Her voice unfurls. Her art ignites. Her business surges. Her love overflows. Because creation flows through authenticity. Because leadership flows through intimacy with your own being. Because power flows through roots, not performance.

Look at a great oak tree, how it stretches wide and high, sheltering and feeding and adding beauty to the world. But none of that is possible without its deep, unseen roots weaving into the Earth. It is the unseen that gives rise to the seen. It is the rootedness that allows the tree to grow strong, weather every storm, to blossom every season, to give generously without collapsing.

You are that tree. You are that force. But first, you must root.

Rooting is the medicine. Rooting is the revolution. Every step you take on the Earth, she supports you. Every breath you take in your body, it holds the memory of your wholeness. You belong. You have always belonged.

It's time to remember. Root into yourself. Root into the Earth. Root into the fire that burns within. From here, you don't just create. From here, you don't just lead. From here, you become a creatrix.

You become a leader of the New Earth.

Unstoppable.

Authentic.

Whole.

Home.

"Rootedness is the revolutionary
act of coming home to every
part of who we are."

What does coming home to myself mean to me right now?

Where in my life do I feel most disconnected from myself?

What parts of me have I shut down or minimized in order to fit in or feel safe? What might it feel like to welcome all parts of myself back together?

How have I prioritized others' needs above my own?

Where do I resist intimacy and raw honesty with myself?

What is my relationship with the word rooted?

How does it feel in my body?

Inanna, Queen of Heaven Portal

Use this Portal to release all that no longer serves you. It's a simple yet powerful gateway to shed the layers of conditioning, priming, and programming that aren't truly you, and that hinder your connection to your authentic self.

Inanna invites you to stand soul-naked.

Strip away what the world has imposed upon you.

Let it all fall to the floor, as if you're undressing.

Allow the identities you've taken on throughout your life to unravel.

Let the armor that guards your innermost self dissolve.

Release the wounding and trauma that cling to your body.

Let your inner child be seen and heard.

Set aside a period of time—perhaps a day or even a week—to experience what it feels like to be soul-naked. Explore who you are in this moment and discover what is truly authentic to you.

Deeper parts of yourself are eager to emerge.

I embark on the journey of self-discovery and integration, guided by the wisdom of Inanna.

As I honor my vulnerability, I reclaim my power and move toward wholeness with love and compassion.

What fears arise when I think about truly rooting into who I am?

What parts of my inner self feel wild, sacred, or powerful but are hidden?

How does resistance show up when I try to slow down and come home to myself?

What outdated programming or beliefs about myself am I ready to release?

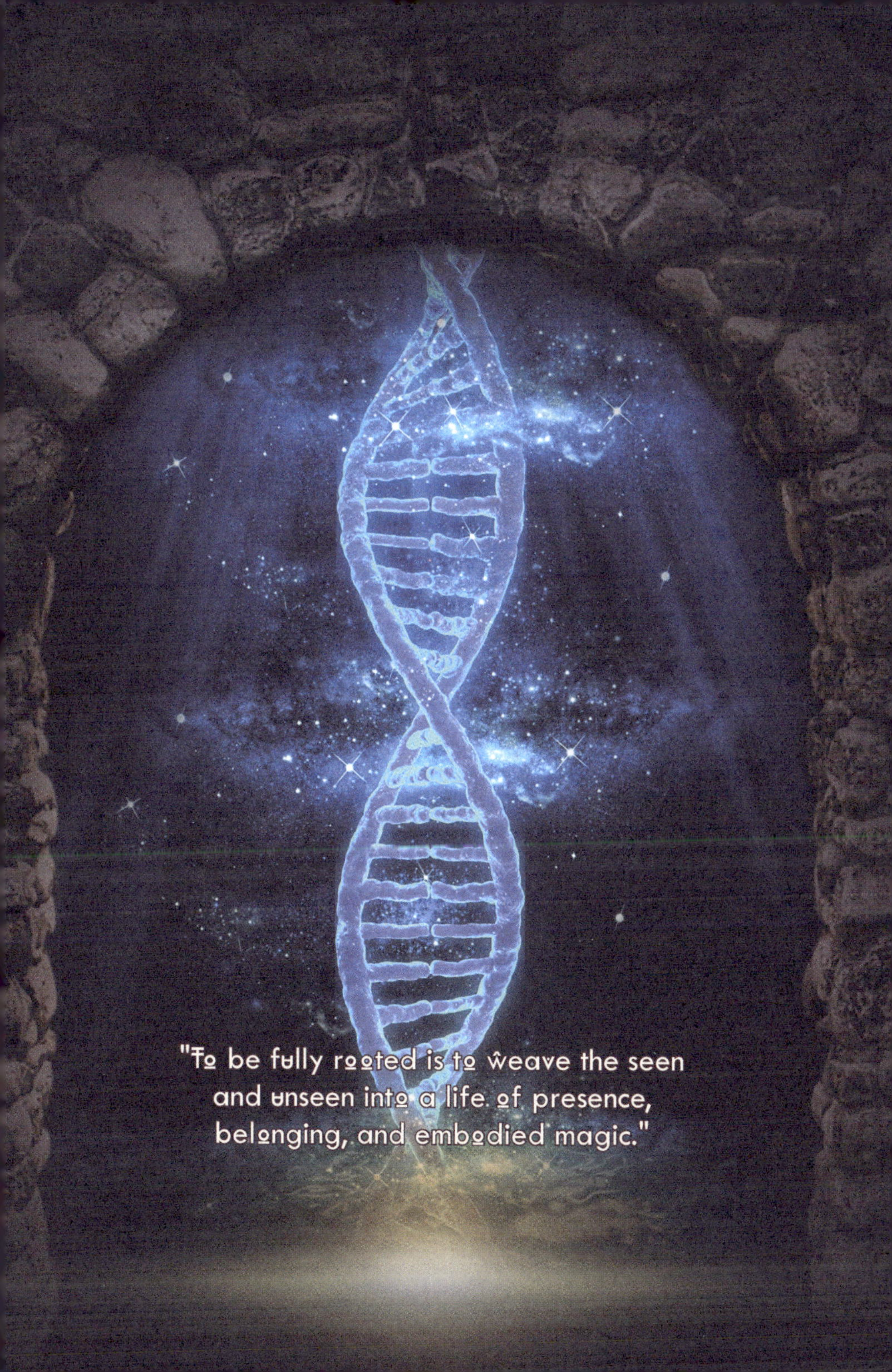
"To be fully rooted is to weave the seen
and unseen into a life of presence,
belonging, and embodied magic."

Rooted Mantras for Coming Home to Yourself

Speak these mantras to integrate and land in your body. Incorporate them into your daily self-care or spiritual practice. Use them as visual anchors in your space, or begin your journaling with them to deepen your transformation.

I come home to myself and honor my body as the sacred temple of my soul.

My rootedness is my revolution. In claiming myself, I reclaim my wholeness.

I ground into Gaia Sophia, and in her embrace, I remember I am endlessly supported.

Through raw honesty and fierce intimacy, I weave all parts of myself back into wholeness.

I let fire alchemize all that is not truly me. I rise—purified, rooted, and free.

What practices help me feel grounded and connected to my body?

What aspects of my true voice and creative expression have been waiting for me to come home to them? What is the true medicine I am here to speak into the world?

What do I need in order to feel fully nourished, grounded, and whole?

What does radical acceptance of all parts of myself look and feel like?

How would my life change if I allowed my full self to be expressed without shame, fear, or guilt?

What outdated beliefs or programming about myself am I ready to release?

A Rooted Story: Rising Rooted

Over two decades ago, I was in a season of chaos—three babies under three, midwifery school, a healing center, a shamanic healing practice, livestock on our ranch, and my coaching business just beginning to move online. I was knee-deep in my shamanic initiations and building a life that, while sacred, was stretching me beyond my capacity.

Every new milestone—a birth, a test, a client surge, a speaking opportunity—sent me spiraling deeper into a feeling I couldn't shake: scattered. No matter how much I accomplished, I couldn't find my center. Until one day, everything cracked open.

After being up for three days straight with sick babies who had, by some miracle, all fallen asleep at once, I walked out into the dusty Colorado land outside our house. I didn't plan it. I didn't think it through. My body just knew. I dropped to the ground, pressed my palms into the earth, and whispered a prayer I didn't know I needed:

Mother of us all, help me carry what I can't. Steady me. Nurture me.
Hold me when I forget how to hold myself.

And then, I felt Her. The Earth. The pulse of her heart. The fierce love. It rushed through my body like lightning. My eyes welled up—not from exhaustion, but from finally feeling held.

No one told me to do it. No ritual. No guided meditation. Just instinct. Just devotion. Just the deep, raw need to root into something ancient and alive.

That day, I remembered something I never want you to forget: <u>You are not meant to carry it all alone.</u>

She is always there. Gaia Sophia. Pachamama. The original mother. The land Herself.

If you're feeling scattered, overwhelmed, spun out—stop. Go outside. Put your hands in the dirt. Press your bare feet to the ground. Let your words, your prayer, your ache rise up. You don't need the perfect script. Your longing is the ritual. The Earth always answers.

This is your reminder: there is a direct path from scattered to rooted. And it's been waiting for you.

Rooted Mantras for Radical Self-Acceptance

Speak these mantras to integrate and activate self-acceptance. Add them into your daily self-care and spiritual practices. Use them as visual anchors in your space or start your journaling practice with them to deepen your transformation.

My belonging begins within. I am already whole, already worthy, already home.

As my roots deepen into the earth, my branches stretch effortlessly toward the cosmos.

The more I root into my truth, the more powerfully my voice, my gifts, and my medicine flow.

I surrender old stories and identities to the flames, making space for my truest self to lead.

Each step I take on this earth is a prayer of gratitude for the sacred support of life itself.

"Our bodies are not just vessels—they are sacred temples through which our soul expresses itself."

Brigid, Goddess of Fire Portal

Use this portal to reconnect with the Earth and Her sacred waters. Your body remembers. Your spark is ready to ignite.

Close your eyes and imagine standing in Ireland, your bare feet planted on the dark green, grassy earth.

Breathe in and draw up the pulsing life force from the land and the Earth Herself.

Let it rise into your body, filling you completely, then radiating outward into your energy field.

Now, place both hands over your heart and feel the flame within—expanding through your body and into your field.

Then, imagine standing before one of Brigid's holy wells.

Reach out and touch the cool, flat stones—an ancient portal to the sacred water.

Dip one hand into the water.

Bring that hand to your third eye, your throat, your heart, and your womb.

You've received a blessing and an attunement from Brigid.

I honor the flame within,
nurturing it with
reverence and
assurance, guided by the
timeless wisdom of
Brigid, Goddess of Fire.

What does it mean to claim my belonging, and where do I still feel I don't belong?

How do I envision my personal roots—where do they extend, and what do they connect me to?

What ancient feminine wisdom feels alive within me?

"Every barefoot step on the Earth is a reminder that we are endlessly supported and deeply loved. She holds, nurtures, and reminds us we already belong."

How does rootedness relate to my ability to create, lead, and express?

What sensations arise in my body when I imagine grounding deeply into the Earth?

How do I honor my multidimensional self while remaining deeply connected to this human experience?

If I could fully trust myself, what bold move or expression would I allow to unfold?

Where can I be more tender, intentional, and reverent with my body, heart, and spirit?

What old stories, masks, or identities am I willing to release in order to root more deeply into my authentic self?

"True creation and leadership
begin the moment we get
radically honest and fiercely
intimate with ourselves."

How can I allow Mother Earth, Gaia Sophia, to hold and support me more fully in my daily life?

Where in my life do I resist receiving support, and how can I open to it with greater trust?

How can I cultivate a more loving, reciprocal relationship with the Earth in my healing and transformation journey?

Invocation for Rooting Deep

Stand with your feet on the Earth, eyes closed, face turned to the sun. Speak this invocation aloud, with conviction.

I call myself back—raw, whole, unapologetic.

I reclaim every piece, every part of me that was silenced, shamed, or forgotten.

I root into this body, this temple, this fierce, holy ground that no longer waits for permission.

I cast off every lie, every mask, every broken story that said I had to be small to be safe.

Grandfather Fire, burn through my veils. Purify what is false. I rise from your flames, unrecognizable to my former self.

Mother Gaia, anchor me. Hold my wild heart steady. Let me feel your ancient knowing in my bones.

I will no longer abandon myself.

I root deep into my soul's knowing, and from this place, I dare to be unstoppable.

I remember who I am.

I am not here to ask for a seat at the table.

I am here to build a whole new world with my bare hands and my unbreakable spirit.

Every step I take is claimed. Every word I speak is sovereign.

I am rooted. Wild. Awake.

I am the slingshot, the quantum force, the living temple of creation.

I rise now—fierce, lit from within.

Creatrix. Leader. Embodied.

What parts of myself still feel unseen, unaccepted, or unloved?

If my body were a sacred temple, how would I care for it differently?

Chapter Two

LIBERATED

"Real liberation is a thousand micro-choices a day."

PRAYER FOR LIBERATED POWER

I choose myself, fully, fiercely, now.

I explore deeper than ever before.

I rise higher into my own becoming.

I expand wider than old stories allow.

Every breath is a prayer for my liberation.

Every step is an act of creation unleashed.

I move forward, awake, alive, unstoppable.

It begins today.

THE INVITATION

You didn't land here by accident. If you are holding this journal, reading these words, then you already know—even if you haven't fully admitted it to yourself yet—that you are a wayshower. A sacred rebel. A divine disruptor. A trailblazer of our times. You didn't come here to play small. You didn't incarnate into this shifting, volatile, breathtaking moment in Earth's story just to blend into the wallpaper and quietly pass into history. You came here to light fires.

This chapter is about full-spectrum liberation. Not the kind you just talk about, not the cookie-cutter kind that fits neatly into an Instagram quote. This is about the real thing—the bone-deep, soul-rattling kind that rips the masks off and burns the old scripts from the center of your being. This is about becoming the multidimensional, cosmic, embodied Goddess that you are—no edits, no filters, no apologies.

Inside of you, there are libraries of wisdom. Rivers of story. Mountains of memories. You have lived not only for yourself but for generations—past, present, and future. Your stories, even the ones you think are too messy, too shameful, too small to matter, are literal gold. They are the medicine. They are the bridge. And stepping into your full liberation means understanding: you are the main character of your story. No more waiting for someone else to crown you, to discover you, to choose you. You are it. You are the one.

Once we root back into ourselves, the next sacred step is liberation. Real liberation isn't a lightning bolt that strikes once and fixes everything. It's a thousand micro-choices a day. It's choosing to interrupt the old patterns. It's refusing to outsource your worth. It's allowing yourself to be messy, tender, feral, expansive—all of it. Choosing yourself over and over again is the revolution.

You are not here at this moment in history by mistake. You chose this time, this wild, chaotic, extraordinary moment, because you are equipped for it. You are one of the sacred architects of the new era, what I call the Age of Sophia. Our consciousness has been accelerating, rising, shifting since long before we were born—from the 1800s' awakening stirrings, through the roaring speed of the 1920s, to the Harmonic Convergence of 1987, through Y2K, through 2012, and now here, at the brink. You can feel it. The Earth's resonance has shifted. Solar flares increased. New templates are flooding in. Everything in the sky, the soil, and our very cells is vibrating faster.

The ancients knew this time would come. They wrote it in their calendars, painted it on their walls, coded it into their myths. A massive paradigm shift. And guess what? You are the shift. Not by default—by choice. And that choice requires your liberation.

Your liberation isn't just for you. It is a ripple across timelines. It is a healing for your ancestors. A permission slip for your descendants. A blessing for the Earth Herself. Every internal chain you break, every lie you shed, every truth you speak out loud sends shockwaves into the collective field.

If you look around and think, "There's nothing I can do," think again. Every external problem that irks you—injustice, fear, manipulation, suppression—has roots inside the human experience and inside your consciousness. And when you heal the part of yourself still carrying the residue, the pattern, you are literally dismantling the structure of that problem on an energetic level.

Healing yourself heals the world.

And here's the thing: learning, growing, liberating—it's cyclical, not linear. Industrialism and toxic patriarchy tried to flatten us into straight lines, into "one and done" narratives. But your liberation, like everything else natural and real, is spiral-natured. Like the seasons. Like the womb. Like the stars.

You don't root once and you're done. You don't liberate once and call it a day. You circle back again and again, deepening, expanding, reclaiming more and more of yourself.

Rooting is your anchor. Liberation is your wings.

This next step, this chapter, is about moving beyond survival. Beyond fitting in. Beyond "good enough." It's about unfurling your cosmic self here, in your body, on this Earth, right now. It's about choosing your authentic voice, your natural creative process, your way of leading and living—even when it looks nothing like the success we're primed with on social media.

It's about saying no to the noise, to the scripts, to the copy-paste reality that was never built for your soul in the first place.

It's about asking yourself every day: What is mine to say today? What is mine to create today? What part of my soul wants to breathe through me today?

I know this path because I've lived it. I've clawed my way out of suffocating expectations. I've burned down the pretty cages they built around me. I've said "no more" to living someone else's story. And yes, it took a lot. Yes, it was messy. Yes, it was the best damn thing I've ever done. And so is your liberation. It won't be neat. It won't be easy. But it will be holy. It will be a homecoming.

You will rise wilder, realer, and more rooted than you ever thought possible. You will move through fear into freedom. Through shedding into sovereignty. Through vulnerability into a breathtaking power that doesn't come from domination, but from deep, sacred alignment with who you actually are.

Every choice matters. Every no to the old opens a yes to the new. Every day you choose to be loyal to your own soul, you rewrite reality for humanity and beyond.

This is the liberation chapter. This is where you breathe deeper. Stand taller. Create louder. Love harder. Lead differently. This is where you free yourself and roar your way into your rightful place in the Age of Sophia.

You ready?
Let's go.

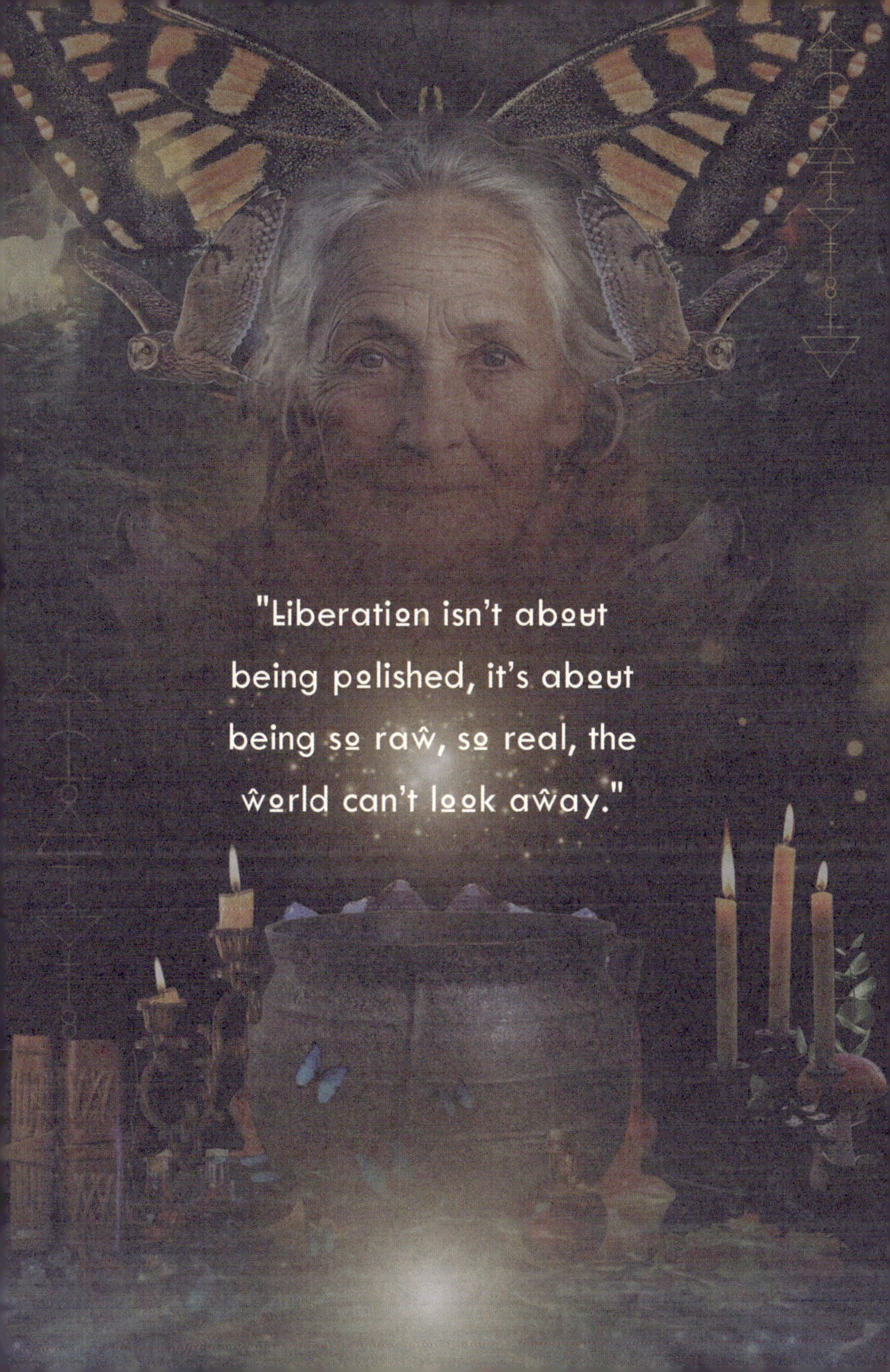
"Liberation isn't about
being polished, it's about
being so raw, so real, the
world can't look away."

What is one bold action I can take today to embody my liberation more fully?

If I stopped waiting for permission, what would I create or say right now?

What old script or story am I ready to burn to ash today?

How would I show up differently if I trusted my wildness as holy?

What piece of my true self am I ready to unveil to the world without apology?

Where have I been holding myself back without even realizing it?

Liberated Mantras for Self-Expression

Speak these mantras to integrate and land in your body. Add them into your daily self-care and spiritual practices. Use them as visual anchors in your space or start your journaling practice with them to deepen your transformation.

I root deeper, rise higher, and liberate louder every single day.

I am the fire that burns through old paradigms and births the new.

I do not wait to be chosen. I choose myself. I crown myself.

Every breath I take is a revolution in devotion to my truest self.

I shed old skins without apology. I am here to evolve, not to please.

Where am I still living by someone else's rules?

What does full-spectrum liberation feel like in my body?

Initiatrix Portal

Use this Portal to connect with the energy around and within you, to feel it viscerally. This portal reminds you of your interconnectedness and your role as a guiding light.

Close your eyes and take two big breaths.

Breathe in through your nose and out through your mouth.

Put your arms up and face palms out, away from you.

For one minute, focus on feeling the currents of life around you—from your own body, house, family, out to your town, social media, world happenings.

Then for the next minute, expand your awareness to the cosmos, your star families, ancient civilizations and ascended masters, and the history held by Mama Gaia—all timelines beyond our knowing, even.

Now bring that awareness back to yourself—your body, your breath.

You are a point of light amidst the beautiful chaos, the beacon of becoming and rebirth.

I embody my role as Initiatrix, trusting in my willingness to evolve, my fluency in navigating change, and my emergence as a beacon of transformation in my life and in the world.

Where do I fear being “too much,” and
what if that’s exactly my medicine?

How have I silenced my own voice in subtle or obvious ways?

"You are the prayer, the prophecy, and the ansŵer - ŵrapped in skin, beating ŵith the ŵild pulse of the future."

What old identities or labels am I ready to shed?

What does it mean for me to be the main character of my own story?

What inner gold am I still hiding from the world?

How have my so-called "flaws" actually been sources of my power?

A Liberated Story: The Birth of Self-Trust

When I had my first baby, I thought I was simply stepping into motherhood. I didn't know I was also stepping into my power.

I'd already had glimpses of liberation. At 14 years old, I said "no" for the first time in my life. A spiritual awakening lit something in me that had been buried under layers of masking and people-pleasing.

But it wasn't until the birth of my son, now 25, that I experienced a full-body, immovable, sovereign no.

After a long 24-hour labor that nearly became a C-section, my son was born and placed on oxygen. That night, I went into the nursery to see him, and though the nurse told me he didn't have a fever, everything in my body said otherwise. I held him in my arms, and he felt warm—too warm. At that time, I still hadn't fully learned to trust myself. I'd spent years second-guessing my instincts, believing others knew better—even about me.

But that night was different.

I asked again. Another nurse came in, double-checked, and sure enough, he did have a fever. Their first thermometer was wrong.

And that beautiful nurse looked me in the eyes and said words I've never forgotten:
"Don't ever go against your intuition. You are always right."

That moment rewired something in me.

Since then, when I've come to new edges, stretched into leadership, or faced moments of doubt, I've returned to that memory. To that knowing. To that sovereign, unwavering no. The one that comes from the body, the heart, the womb—not the mind's logic, but the deep compass of truth within.

So, if you're reading this and still wrestling with self-trust, this is your reminder: Your intuition is never wrong. Your body knows. Start listening, start honoring, and life will rise up to meet your power.

You were born to trust yourself. You were born to lead.

"We don't come here to fit in, we come here to liberate all parts of ourselves and live as the full-spectrum beings we are."

What does fierce, embodied leadership look like for me?

What does the Age of Sophia
awaken inside of me?

What frequency am I committed to weaving into this new era?

How can I embody my own medicine more deeply each day?

What does sacred rebellion look like in my life right now?

What story within me is asking to be honored, healed, and shared?

How do I honor both my wildness and my wisdom?

Liberated Mantras for Intentional Bravery

Speak these mantras to integrate and activate self-acceptance. Add them into your daily self-care and spiritual practices. Use them as visual anchors in your space or start your journaling practice with them to deepen your transformation.

My voice is sacred. My truth is sovereign.
My soul is unrelenting.

I honor every part of my story, the gold,
the grit, the becoming.

I will not water myself down to soothe a
world afraid of its own awakening.

I am wild, holy, and whole.

My freedom heals not only me - it heals
timelines, lineages, and the Earth Herself.

"You're not lost. You're not broken. You're remembering your power, and that remembrance is liberation itself."

How is my body guiding me toward my next evolution?

How have I been dimming my own sacred fire?

What are the anchors that keep me rooted in my truth?

What would change if I lived from my full multidimensionality?

Wild Persephone Portal

Use this Portal to access and unearth the multidimensional, full spectrum version of you, liberated and ready to share who you are with the world.

Center yourself with your breath.

Visualize a cord extending from your tailbone, down through many layers of earth and rock, all the way to the center of Mother Earth, anchoring into Her green Tourmaline core.

Stay connected to Her energy.

Feel the season of summer, the warmth of the sun, the sounds of moving water, plants in full bloom, and the easefulness of lazy days.

Next, feel the season of fall, the cool, crisp air that turns you inward to gather, savor, and experience the abundance of fruition.

Then, dive deep into the season of winter. Full cozy-up-by-the-fire vibes, restoration, dreaming, and the stillness of the void.

Last, feel the emergence of spring, fresh, increasing energy, renewal, and the tending of the new.

Feel how each of these seasons lives within you, and reflect on your unique expression of them.

Explore which seasons need more integration in your life, and which you may hold limitations or judgments about.

"Your story, even the
parts you hide away, is
literal gold. It holds
medicine for others and
for the world."

Where do I still seek safety over sovereignty?

What sacred "no" am I being called to say?

What energy do I want my days to be rooted in?

How can I create a life that reflects my inner liberation?

Invocation for Wholehearted Liberation

Stand with your feet on the Earth, eyes closed with your face turned to the sun. Speak this invocation aloud, with conviction.

I stand here, no masks, no pretending, at the edge of my own evolution.
I call back every piece of me I left behind to survive.
I gather every part of me, the bold, the tender, the feral,
into this moment.
I am not waiting.
I am not seeking permission.
I am not asking who I'm allowed to become.
I choose myself now, fully, wildly, unapologetically.
I choose the deeper rooting.
I choose the full expression.
I choose the expansion, even when it demands I leave old skins behind.
I am here to live, not perform.
I am here to create, not fit in.
I am here to experience everything my soul came for, the ache, the rising, the becoming.
Every breath I take now feeds my future.
Every choice I make now liberates generations.
Every time I trust myself, I move the world forward.
I am not who I was yesterday.
I am not done growing, and I never will be.
I walk forward, fierce, open, alive, choosing who I am becoming with every single step.
It begins now.
It begins with me.

How can I honor the seasons and spirals of my own becoming? What new rhythms am I being called to live by?

Where am I being asked to lead, even if it feels uncomfortable?

Chapter Three

EXPRESSED

"Every messy word, every imperfect offering, every breath of your truth shatters old paradigms and seeds new worlds."

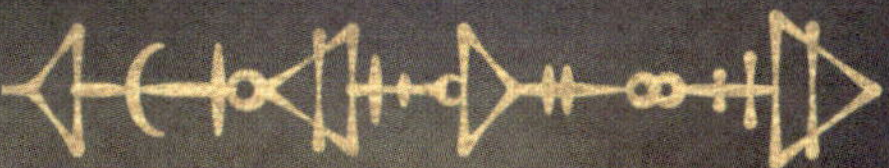

A PRAYER FOR HOLY EXPRESSION

I call back every silenced word.

Every caged dream.

Every breath held too long.

I root into my wild frequency.

I rise through the mess.

I trust the flood.

I offer my raw, holy self as medicine to the world.

I choose now.

I choose all of me.

I express.

THE INVITATION

Welcome to the turning point. The moment where everything you have worked for—rooting in, liberating yourself, calling all your parts home—now asks to be brought forward.

This chapter is about expression, and I don't mean the fake, sanitized, pre-approved, airbrushed expression we're sold by a culture addicted to performance. I mean the raw, holy, cracked-open, can't-not-speak-it expression of your living frequency. I mean the art of being seen, of being felt, of letting your very beingness become a transmission in the world.

Most people never get here. They root a little. They liberate a little. But when it comes to actually standing up, opening their mouth, writing the book, taking the stage, letting themselves be received? They get swallowed by the noise. By the conditioning. By the ancient, bone-deep fear of "Who am I to speak? Who am I to create? Who am I to lead?"

And that, right there, is why this chapter matters so much.
Expression is your sacred offering. It's not just about talking louder. It's about embodying who you are so fully that your presence alone becomes medicine. Your life becomes a living offering. Your frequency becomes a gift you place into the hands of the world.

But to get there? You have to know what expression actually means for you.

For some of you, expression will look like writing that book that's been haunting you for years. For some, it'll be stepping onto a stage. For some, it's finally admitting the thing you've been hiding even from yourself. Expression is personal.

And, if we're being real, expression is programmed against us from the second we arrive here. I can tell you that from experience.

I was four years old, lying on the floor of my grandfather's office, when I said the first thing I truly wanted in life: I want to be a writer. And in that tiny moment, that passion and knowing got shut down. "You can't do that. You'll starve. You'll never make it. Don't even think about it again."

Four years old—and already, my expression was treated like a threat.

You have your own versions of this. The moments when your song, your vision, your words were caged. And that's the thing: they're still trapped in those cages if we don't go in, get messy, and resurrect them.

That's what we're doing here. We're getting real about the programs, the conditions, the deep, toxic ways we've learned to suffocate our own voices. We're not "learning to express," we're unlearning everything that blocked it.

We are remembering.

And it's messy. Expression is messy, wild, untamed. It doesn't always fit into the neat little boxes. It doesn't always sound "right." It doesn't always look pretty. But it is holy. And it is powerful. And it is yours.

Now here's the thing nobody tells you: expression begins with frequency. It's not just about "having something to say." It's about the energy you hold.

If your body is exhausted, if your mind is clogged, if your energy is bleeding out everywhere because you're carrying too much of the wrong energy or you don't have enough of your own energy, your expression can't flow cleanly. It will get distorted. Blocked. Muted.

You have to care for your frequency first. You have to cultivate it. Breathe with it. Ground it into your body. Your frequency IS your message. Your breath. Your health. Your nervous system. Your home. Your daily rituals. Your choices. Your boundaries. All of it is impacting your level of expression.

And when that frequency is clear and strong? You cannot help but create. Ideas will pour through you. Opportunities will magnetize to you. Your words will crack open the world.

Not because you tried harder, but because you became a clear vessel. Expression is a full-body, full-being, full-hearted experience. And you have to protect it. Hold your energy field.

Too many women lose themselves the moment they try to "express." They look sideways. They compare. They scroll until they're so saturated in everyone else's frequency that they forget their own.

Not here. Not anymore.

You will stand in your own frequency like a living rose, rooted and radiant. You will commune, not consume. You will share energy, not lose yourself in it. You are not here to be a thousand watered-down versions of somebody else. You are here to be you. Fully. Fiercely. Freely.

This path asks for a blend of the sacred masculine and the sacred feminine. It asks for structures that hold you, and the mystic, surrendered space for creation to rush through you.
You need both. You need to be both the river and the riverbed.

And you have to let it get messy. You have to be willing to let your ideas crash over you like waves, not knowing where they will land. You have to let the inspiration flood through you and trust you can sort it out later. Because when you do? You enter the state where magic happens. Where the divine moves through you. Where you create projects, books, businesses, art, communities—things that leave trails of light behind you, long after you're gone.

That is legacy. That is leadership. That is the power of true expression.

And make no mistake, when you commit to being fully expressed, you change not just your life, but the trajectory of the collective. Your expression ripples out. It creates new timelines. It shatters old paradigms. It seeds the world with possibility and new levels of consciousness.

You were made for this.

You didn't root and liberate yourself just to hide. You didn't do all that deep work just to sit in the wings. You came here to live, to create, to lead.

And that starts with saying yes to your own expression. Not later. Not when it's perfect. Not when you feel "ready."

Now. Messy. Beautiful. Powerful. Let it pour through you. Let yourself be seen, heard, felt. Free to be expressed.

"Expression isn't clean or pretty,
it's wild, holy, cracked open,
and unapologetically yours."

Where am I still playing small with my expression?

What does it mean for me to be a living transmission?

When did I first feel my voice get caged?

What old programming still tries to silence me?

What is the ŵild, raŵ expression inside me aching to be freed?

What feels too “messy” to share, and why?

Where am I still waiting for permission to speak?

What does sacred, cracked-open expression look like for me?

Lady of the Lake Portal

Use this portal to step into the sacred mist. Strip away the noise, the programming, the false identities. Reclaim your raw, unshakable essence and rise as the pure, untamed frequency you were born to be.

Close your eyes and feel yourself seated on the bench of a small wooden boat adrift on the cool, misty sacred lake.

Your hands hold onto the smooth sides of the boat as the water sloshes gently along the boat and you float further into the thick mist.

Breathe.

Listen to the sound of the water.

Soak in the silence, clarity, and fluency of this place.

The tangible energy of magic abounds.

You are by yourself, but not alone.

You are in the presence of profound support here.

Feel who you are in this space, the essence at the very core of your being.

Take this with you into the world.

Your expression unfolds here, sister.

I surrender to the depths
of my inner magic,
expressing my true
essence with fearless
authenticity, guided by
the mystical wisdom of
the Lady of the Lake.

Where am I still leaking my energy to the noise of others?

What part of me is still trying to fit in and perform?

If I ŵas free from judgment, ŵhat ŵould I create first?

What frequency do I want to pour into the world?

"Your frequency is your message. Your breath, your body, your boundaries are the sacred keepers of your voice."

Expressed Mantras for Unleashing Your Sacred Voice

Speak these mantras to integrate and land in your body, add them into your daily self-care and spiritual practices. Use them as visual anchors in your space or start your journaling practice with them to deepen your transformation.

My voice is a living transmission.

I create without waiting for permission.

My truth is messy, holy, and real.

I am a vessel for divine expression.

My voice is ancient, wild, and sovereign.

If my body is my instrument of expression,
what does it need today?

What sacred structures (routines, rituals) would support my fullest expression?

How am I tending (or neglecting) my sacred expression?

Where am I still outsourcing my worth in subtle ways?

What parts of my story still feel too raw to tell, and what if they are my real medicine?

A Liberated Story: The Unscripted Edge

In the early 2000s, my world was bursting at the seams. I was running a healing center, raising three babies under three, leading community shamanic bowl ceremonies, and starting to speak on stages. People began flying in from other states to work with me. Big-name speakers showed up in my small-town healing center. My herbal store was selling out faster than I could make medicines. I was nursing babies while I spoke on stages, and choosing with discernment, because I wasn't willing to leave my children for just anything and never for more than a few hours.

I'd always been a performer - singing, dancing, acting, piano, ballet. So when I was first invited to speak, I chose a local event not knowing I was about to meet my creative edge. I walked on stage, and blacked out. Not in a bad way, just in a channeling way. It wasn't new. I'd done it all my life performing, just not yet speaking or unpracticed. But this time, I recognized it for what it was: a full-body surrender to creation. I channeled the entire talk - bowls, story, message, ways to work with me - and came back to reality at the end, lit up.

People asked, "How can you go on stage with no notes? How do you not know what you said?" My answer: I trust myself. I trust creation. I trust the co-creative forces that move through me, my higher self, ancestors, the women in the room, the unseen ones who walk with me.

Creation isn't about control. It's about communion and opening to the flow of what wants to come through you.

Over the years, I honed this gift. I even had people transcribe my talks so I could read what came through afterward. I became a sought-after speaker - not because I had polished scripts or was an eloquent speaker, but because I brought truth, medicine, and real-time activation.

If you feel the call to speak, create, or lead, but you're scared and excited at the same time - that's your GO sign. That means something big wants to move through you. You don't need to have it all figured out. You just need to say yes.

Speak. Share. Trust.

Because what is yours to share, only you can bring. And that's where the revolution begins.

"Expression is a full-
body initiation. It
demands all of you,
messy, magnificent,
untamed."

How can I hold myself when my creative river floods its banks?

What energy am I breathing into my creations right now?

How do I commune with the divine when I create?

What ancient parts of myself are ready to resurrect and roar forward?

Expressed Mantras for Raw Creativity

Speak these mantras to integrate and activate self-acceptance, add them into your daily self-care and spiritual practices. Use them as visual anchors in your space or start your journaling practice with them to deepen your transformation.

I am a clear vessel, fierce, grounded, and overflowing.

I am not here to blend in, I'm here to create.

I trust my wild creative flood.

Messy expression is sacred, I let it pour through me.

I surrender to my raw, uncensored, mystical expression.

What would it feel like to create without needing it to be "worth something"?

What parts of my expression have I been hiding, apologizing for, or downplaying?

What vision is knocking at the door of my heart and am I willing to answer?

What does it mean to be the medicine instead of just offering it?

"You didn't come here to
perform perfection. You
came here to embody
the full aliveness of your
sacred, feral soul."

Magdelana of the Rose Portal

Use this Portal to enter the spell of the Rose. Breathe her in, trace her thorns, and let her fierce, ancient magic awaken the unapologetic truth sleeping in your bones. Anchor into your sovereign authority and expression.

Close your eyes and breathe deeply.

Take your biggest breath possible, and let it out with an audible sigh.

Visualize holding a fully open red rose.

See it in all its lush, velvety layers, intricately spiraling into its center.

Smell its sweet scent.

Now run your fingers down its stem to carefully feel the thorns.

The rose comes to you today to commune.

To take you in and to be taken in by you.

The rose is delicate, beautiful and powerful all at the same time.

Ask her what message she has for you today.

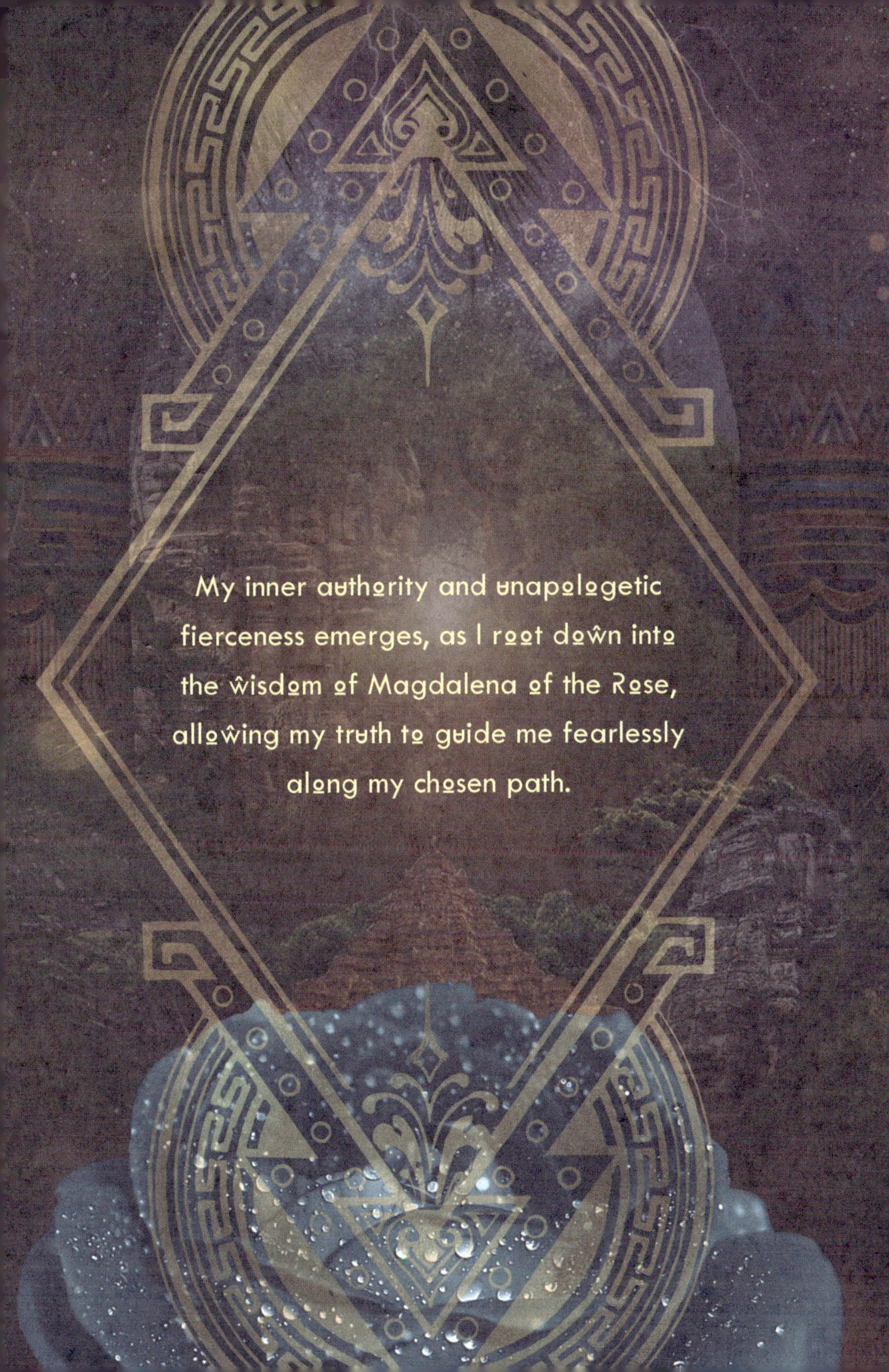
My inner authority and unapologetic
fierceness emerges, as I root down into
the wisdom of Magdalena of the Rose,
allowing my truth to guide me fearlessly
along my chosen path.

"The world doesn't need
another polished clone. It needs
the raw, unfiltered revolution
that only you can bring."

What legacy do I want my raw expression to leave behind?

Where have I been holding back the truest, wildest parts of my expression, and why?

What old programming or fear still whispers that my voice is a threat?

If my expression could seed new timelines and ripple through the collective, what do I most want to say?

Invocation for Untamed Expression

Stand with your feet on the Earth, eyes closed with your face turned to the sun. Speak this invocation aloud, with conviction.

I stand at the turning point, the threshold where my beingness demands to be expressed.

I refuse the fake performance sold to us.

I am here for the raw, cracked-open, holy expression.

I'm here for my living frequency.

I am not here to be muted, minimized, or molded.

I am the transmission.

I am the medicine.

I am the frequency that will not be caged.

Today, I remember: Expression is not about volume, it's about embodiment.

It's not about waiting, it's about rising, now.

I claim my sacred right to be seen, heard, and felt.

I will not get swallowed by noise.

I will not abandon my voice to conditioning.

I am a clear vessel, not because I tried harder, but because I became.

I hold my field like a living rose, rooted and radiant.

I commune, not consume.

I lead, not follow.

I trust my mess, my magic, my storm.

I say yes to the legacy I was
born to create.

Not someday.

Not when it's perfect.

Now.

Messy. Beautiful. Powerful.

Expressed.

What sacred structure or daily ritual could help me hold my frequency stronger while creating?

What would my life look like if I lived as a full-body, full-frequency transmission every single day?

Chapter Four
FIERCE
“Sovereignty doesn’t whisper.
It leads.”

PRAYER FOR SOVEREIGN LEADERSHIP

I stand at the threshold of legacy.

Fierce and sovereign.

I cast off all false roles.

I rise as the architect of new timelines.

May my voice be truth.

May my presence be power.

May my life be a living offering.

I lead with heart, fire, and unapologetic devotion.

THE INVITATION

This is it. The final turn in the spiral. The moment where everything we've journeyed through, the rooting, the reclamation, the ripping off of old skins, starts to crystallize into something far greater: legacy. Not in the fluffy, performative, "how will I be remembered" kind of way. No. This chapter is about your living legacy. The frequency you embody right now. The decisions you make right now. The truth you lead with right now.

Let's get real: you can't lead others until you can fully, fiercely lead yourself. Self-leadership isn't a concept. It's a daily devotion. It's every moment you choose to trust yourself over the noise. It's choosing integrity when shortcuts look easier. It's having the guts to speak when staying silent would be safer. Every ripple outward begins inside. This is the unshakable foundation of true legacy.

Leadership in this new paradigm is not about hierarchy. We're not here to rule from above. We're here to rise together. To dismantle the old, extract the poison, and infuse leadership with presence, with purpose, with truth. We lead not by being louder, but by being truer. We don't need titles. We don't need crowns. Our sovereignty lives in our cells.

Real power? It's not domination. It's responsibility. It's the ability to hold your energy, your truth, your medicine, in a way that brings others home to themselves. When you stand in your sovereign power, you become a sacred disruptor. You shake the ground, not for attention, but because your presence demands alignment. This kind of leadership is not safe. It's not palatable. It doesn't beg for permission. It births new eras and greater awakenings.

And here's the truth most won't tell you: legacy isn't something you leave behind. It's something you live into every day. It's how you mother. How you serve. How you create. How you love. How you dare to stay rooted in who you are when the world keeps trying to water you down.

It means choosing your frequency over performance. Your body over burnout. Your truth over approval.

Legacy is not about dependency. It's not about clinging to your creations. It's about building something that can be handed off, that lives beyond you. Something that moves with its own heartbeat. Something that ripples across generations. This is your movement. Your revolution. Your medicine.

But to get there, you have to lead yourself there. You have to stop minimizing your knowing. You have to burn down the fear of being too much. You have to claim your audacity.

No more shrinking. No more apologizing. No more waiting to be chosen. You are already the leader. You are already the legacy.

So this chapter? It asks more of you. More courage. More clarity. More commitment.

Because the truth is, you shape the future by how you choose to live now.

Welcome to the chapter where the fire gets fierce. Where your sovereignty takes center stage. Where your legacy comes alive.

“You are already the legacy.

Now live like it.”

What does self-leadership mean to me, and am I truly living it daily?

What outdated leadership models am I ready to burn down?

How does my energy lead before I even speak?

Where in my life am I still waiting for permission?

What truth am I avoiding because it feels too big to hold?

How do I show up when no one is watching?

What legacy am I actively building through my daily choices?

Priestess of Atlantis Portal

Use this portal to enter the depths with the Priestess of Atlantis to unlock ancient wisdom, awaken your true power, and reclaim the self-mastery and energetic wealth that fuel your sacred leadership and service.

Close your eyes and envision diving beneath the tumultuous surface of the Atlantic ocean.

You are guided down, down, down into the depths by the Priestess of Atlantis.

The sunlight is dim here, you continue to follow her through a huge arch of an underwater ruin.

You are time shifting through the corridors of time to the time of Atlantis.

She turns to you and speaks, "Here you will remember."

She stays with you.

Feel into the space, open to ancient memories and wisdom from this era - they are keys to your self-mastery.

What do you feel?

When you are done here, travel back through time and rise back up to the surface and breathe.

Atlantis remains in the hearts of all who remember.

I embrace my power with wisdom and balance. I wield my abilities with integrity and compassion, knowing that true strength lies in self-mastery.

What am I most afraid people will see if I show up fully?

How do I bring others home to themselves just by being me?

Fierce Mantras for Sovereignty

Speak these mantras to integrate and land in your body, add them into your daily self-care and spiritual practices. Use them as visual anchors in your space or start your journaling practice with them to deepen your transformation.

I lead myself, first, fully, fiercely.

My self-trust is unshakable.

I am the revolution I came for.

My truth shakes the ground and roots new realities.

Sovereignty lives in my cells.

What's one bold decision I've been putting off?

Where am I still seeking approval instead of standing in my truth?

Where am I leading from fear instead of devotion? What would it mean to fully embody sacred disruption?

Where am I still playing small to stay safe?

How am I shaping the future through the way I mother/create/speak/serve?

What am I trying to carry that's not mine?

If my frequency is my legacy, what does it say right now?

A Fierce Story: Born to Lead

I've always found it fascinating - and telling - that so many awakened women, the true leaders and creatrixes of this world, started out as masked, good girls. Highly sensitive. Deeply intuitive. And yet somehow, deeply disconnected from that truth. Conditioned to be small, polite, agreeable. Anything to stay safe in the system that didn't know what to do with our innate sacred rebellion.

For me, the shift began around age 14. I'd spent my childhood in full camouflage, so far from my truth I barely existed as "me." But I started saying no. Slowly at first. Then, a no loud enough to get me sent to boarding school - a supposed punishment that turned out to be liberation.

The real turning point came when I stepped into what was supposed to be a PE class…in a horse corral.

That's where I met Mellow Yellow. The tall, palomino quarter horse that changed my life.

The moment I walked toward him, I felt his heart before I ever touched him. And when we did connect, something ancient and true sparked: My sensitivity wasn't a flaw. It was my power.

Mellow Yellow showed me that feeling deeply, feeling everything, was't something to hide or fear. It was my gift. My magic. My divine service.

Before that moment, I thought being highly sensitive meant I had to shrink. That I couldn't possibly hold the intensity of life, let alone lead inside of it. But this horse, this gentle, steady being, showed me what it looked like to hold immense energy without shutting down. To offer presence and healing without needing words. To radiate unconditional love and power, just by being.

I rode him every day. I eventually bought him, and we barrel raced together for years. We healed together. He helped me remember what was always true: that my leadership would never come from separation, but from deep, embodied connection - to my body, to the Earth, to my feelings, to others.

And so if you're someone who feels deeply, don't shut that down. That sensitivity? It's not just for you. It's your power to move mountains, to shape timelines, to change lives.

You are beautifully built this way for a reason. Your sensitivity and depth aren't burdens, they're precious gifts. If you stay small or hide from life's intensity, you deny the world your medicine. There are people waiting for your truth, your story, your presence. This is your moment to rise, to come alive, to lead from who you truly are. Your impact, your artistry, your legacy, they only grow the more you lean in.

Let the world feel your full, unfiltered heart. We're waiting for it. We're waiting for you.

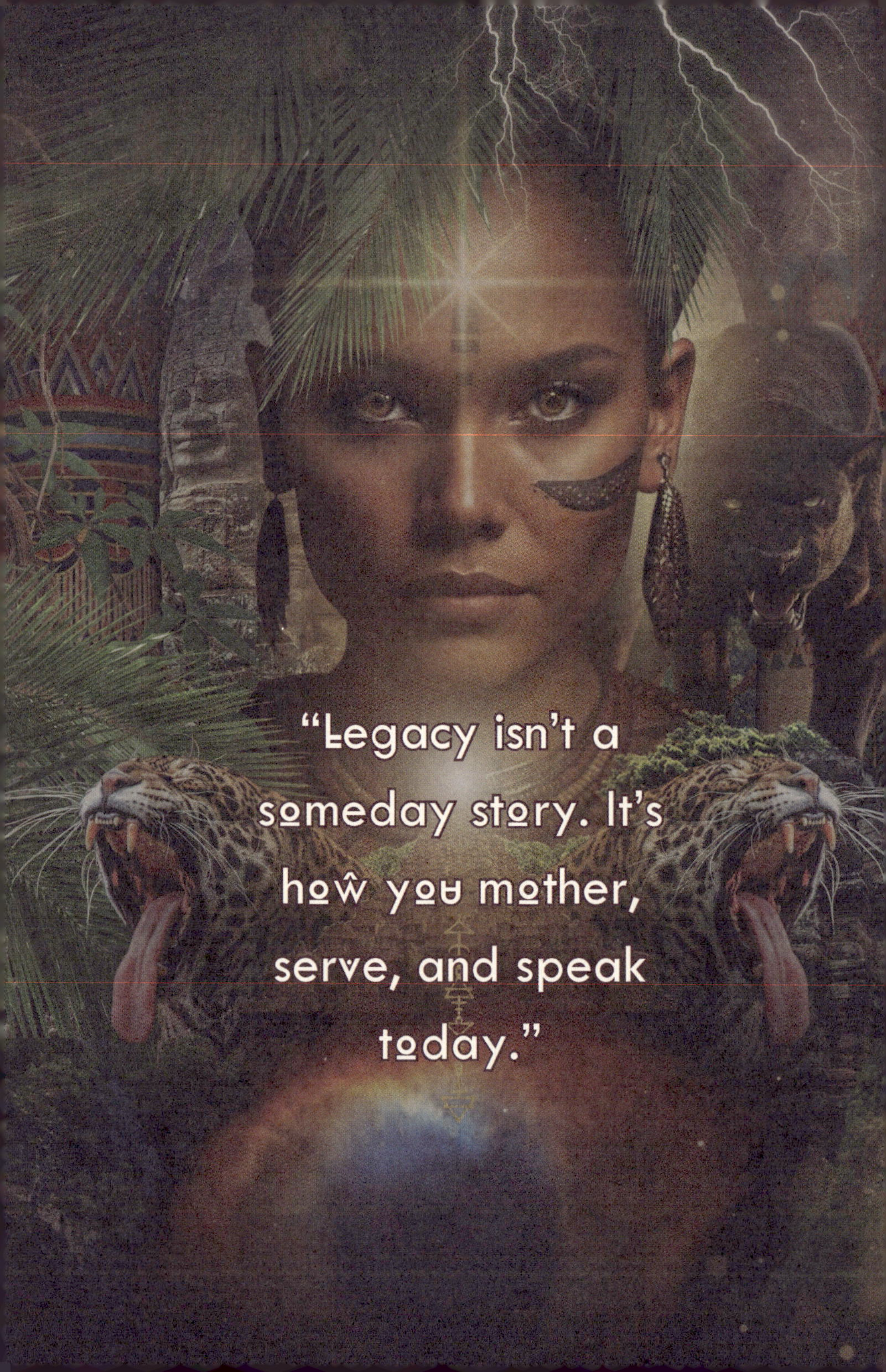
"Legacy isn't a someday story. It's how you mother, serve, and speak today."

Where have I chosen burnout over boundaries, and why?

What story about leadership needs to be rewritten in my life?

What revolution is already living inside me, waiting to lead?

Where do I feel the most powerful and the most free?

What habits or beliefs are no longer aligned with my future?

If I trusted my inner authority, what would I say or do next?

What are the ripple effects of my truth when I don't hold back?

Fierce Mantras for Legacy Keepers

Speak these mantras to integrate and activate self-acceptance, add them into your daily self-care and spiritual practices. Use them as visual anchors in your space or start your journaling practice with them to deepen your transformation.

I am legacy in motion.

I lead because I remember who I am.

Legacy is how I love, serve, and create, right now.

I lead without title, without crown, without apology.

My frequency leads louder than words ever could.

"Leadership doesn't ask
for permission.
It walks in knowing it
belongs."

How does sovereignty feel in my body?

What old leadership wounds or betrayals still influence me?

What am I most proud of that no one sees?

What would I do differently if I knew I couldn't be "too much"?

What systems or structures am I here to dismantle or rebuild?

The Jaguar Council Portal

Use this portal to attune to the Black Jaguar's fierce knowing and embodied power. This portal awakens your sacred role as a revolutionary creator, guiding you to lead, express, and embody your legacy.

Close your eyes and breathe.

The black jaguar stands before you, an ambassador for the role you are meant to step into.

She slowly, deliberately slinks towards you, radiating confidence, unwavering knowingness, and courage for you to attune to.

Feel her embodied energy, the simplicity of her perspective.

She just is who she came here to be.

No trying or stories about why she can't or has to wait to live the role she came here to fulfill.

She is.

Now, she walks with you as a guide to help you expand into your highest potential.

Become Her.

Place something on your altar to remind you of her support and step into the next level of your frequency, creativity and leadership.

I am a Golden Age Revolutionary
birthing the Age of Sophia through my
leadership, embodiment and expression.

"Legacy is not about
being remembered.
It's about being
radically,
unmistakably you,
right now."

What truth have I been swallowing to stay safe, and what would change if I spoke it now?

Invocation for Fierce Sovereignty

Stand with your feet on the Earth, eyes closed with your face turned to the sun. Speak this invocation aloud, with conviction.

I call forward the fiercest part of me now.
The one who's walked through flame after flame.
The one who's rooted deep, ripped off the false skins, reclaimed every exiled part.
The one who's said, "This is mine. This is me."
I stand at the final turn of the spiral.
I'm not looking back to be remembered.
But stepping forward to be felt.
My legacy is not someday, it is now.
It's how I lead myself in the dark.
How I choose truth when silence is safer.
How I rise without title, without permission.
And still hold the power of the storm in my chest.
I invoke the sacred disruptor within me.
The one who doesn't perform, doesn't please, doesn't bow.
I lead from the inside out.
From the core of my knowing.
From the sovereignty in my cells.
From the devotion that refuses to die.
May every breath I take become a ripple.
May every act of courage ignite new timelines.
I do not shrink. I do not wait.
I am the architect of what comes next.
I am the revolution I came here to birth.
I am the leader.
I am the legacy.
Now, let's set the world on fire.

Where am I meant to go first, to light the ŵay for others?

What would my highest self do right now?

Closing Spark

To the woman reading this, thank you. Thank you for doing the real, gritty, luminous work of returning to yourself, of reclaiming your voice, and of stepping into the audacity of your leadership.

You didn't just skim the surface, you went all the way in. You cracked open. You remembered. You burned the old to the ground and chose to rise in your own sacred fire.

This journey we've walked together wasn't light. It was legacy work. And you showed up for it. Fiercely. Unapologetically. That matters more than you know.

You're not just part of the shift, you are the shift. You are on the leading edge of creation, sculpting a future the world has never seen before. One rooted in embodiment, truth, beauty, and bold feminine power. You're not waiting for permission. You're becoming the new blueprint.

If you take nothing else from this journal, take this: the work you've done here ripples. Through your family, your clients, your creations, through time itself. You are part of something so much bigger.

And you're not doing it alone.

We rise because you rise.

We become because you dared to become.

Together, we are the revolution.

With Love, Shannon

Gratitude

Creating this journal has been an initiation - as all my work is. I truly believe when we create from our soul, everyone involved, including the creator herself, is transformed. I'm thankful for being able to share my heart and wisdom to awaken women who are birthing the New Earth through their rising.

Stephanie Wicker-Campbell, your intuitive design genius brought this journal to life in a way only you could. Your patience, creativity, and deep alignment with the vision made every page a sing. It's an honor to keep creating alongside you.

To the sixteen Featured Authors of the Creatrix Awakened Oracle Deck which this journal stems from: your trust, wisdom, and voice made this a sacred collaboration. Thank you for saying yes and showing up with so much heart.

For my mentors, who have lit my creative flame and helped me bring more of myself forward. To Jenna Brown, for her steady support and liberating divergent brilliance she brings to everything she touches. To Ke'oni Hanalei, for his infinite capacity to hold space, and translate ancient medicine into modern embodiment. And to Christy Nault, for rekindling the hope that healing was possible, and for equipping me with the support and sacred plant medicines that helped restore my wholeness.

And to my family - my husband, Brent, my sons Garrett, Aidan, Caleb, and Wesley - you are the soul of everything I create. Brent, thank you for holding it all with love. Boys, thank you for making me brave. You are my why, my center, and my wings.

For all who made this journal possible - you are woven into its pages. This is our legacy.

About the Author

Shannon Van Den Berg is a Shamanic Business and Wealth Mentor, International Bestselling Author multiple times over, and the visionary founder of the Jaguar Leadership Council. A fierce activator of New Earth Feminine Leadership, Shannon has spent over two decades guiding leaders, visionaries, and soul-led entrepreneurs into their highest expression of power, prosperity, and purpose.

As a Sophianic Lemurian Jaguar Rose Priestess, Shannon curates transformational experiences that awaken ancient remembrance and catalyze embodied impact. Her work is a call to rise - to lead, create, and serve from a place of deep soul sovereignty and revolutionary integrity.

Through her mentorship and movement-building work, Shannon supports those who are ready to burn down outdated paradigms and birth the Golden Age through their frequency, leadership, and expression. Her teachings are known to be fiercely loving, unapologetically bold, and deeply rooted in both mystical tradition and grounded action.

Shannon lives in the wild beauty of Hesperus, Colorado in the foothills of the Rocky Mountains, with her husband and their four homeschooled sons. Whether tending to her homestead or embracing her Lemurian roots on the sacred lands and waters of Kauai, she embodies what she teaches - truth, legacy, and the audacity to lead from within.

Discover more about Shannon, explore her other creations, connect with her work, and unlock exclusive gifts for the Creatrix within by scanning this QR code.